DATE DUE			
MAY 22 '7?			
NOV 19 '7?			
MAY 16 '77			
~~FEB 11 '85~~			
MAY 22 '86			
MAR 15 1989			
~~FEB 22 1989~~			
MAR 21 '90			

kids camping

KIDS

CAMPING

by Aileen Paul

illustrated by John Delulio

Doubleday & Company, Inc., Garden City, New York

to all children and young people—
especially to my own: Fred, Katie, Celia, and Walter;
and to their friends, Lisa, Bill, and Chris,
who shared our first camping experiences.

Man – 1039 – c. 1
ISBN: 0-385-02937-3 Trade
        0-385-02939-X Prebound
Library of Congress Catalog Card Number 72-92236
Copyright © 1973 by Doubleday & Company, Inc.
All Rights Reserved
Printed in the United States of America
9   8   7   6   5   4   3   2

contents

Introduction   7

A Word to Kids   9

A Word to Adults   11

1. Planning Your Trip   13
2. Where to Go   16
3. Tents   26
4. Sleeping Bags   35
5. Camp Life: Setting Up, While There, Breaking Camp   40
6. Camp Cooking

    Part 1   50
    Part 2   58
    Part 3   62

7. Suggested Menus and Grocery List for Four People for Seven Days   66
8. Backpacking   87
9. Camping by the Sea   93

10. Camping in Canada   95
11. Camping in Mexico   101
12. Common Sense   106
13. Lists of Things You Will Need   114
14. For More Information   119

Index   124

introduction

The idea for writing KIDS CAMPING grew because we wanted to go camping—my family and I—but we didn't know where to go or what to do.

The more we listened to friends—skilled campers all—discuss the joys and problems of camping, the less we seemed to know about the basic facts of camping.

There was so much to learn, and the learning itself (on our own) was such fun that I decided to share it with you.

KIDS CAMPING is only a beginning book. You will have much to add from your own experience.

a word to kids

Camping is for fun, but the equipment you need and the way in which you use it, is serious business. This book is intended to help you plan what you do and what you need. There are many places and ways to go camping.

As a start, consider where you will go and where you will camp when you get there. The first campground you choose should be reasonably near your home and should contain services such as water and sanitary facilities to make your initial experience easier. A small store in which you can buy forgotten supplies is also helpful.

Wilderness or backpacking trips, I think you will agree after reading this book, should wait until you are an older, more practiced camper. I have, however, included a chapter on backpacking to give you an idea of what can be ahead for you.

In your planning, and before your first trip, allow time for practicing camping skills: set up your tent and take it down; pack and unpack clothing and personal supplies; sleep in your sleeping bag; cook some of the food you have chosen; wear camping clothes, particularly boots or shoes which should be well broken in before you start.

By doing that, you will become more skilled in techniques of camping, and, as you know, the better you are at something, the more fun it is. Another advantage to learning in advance is that more time is available at campsite for swimming, hiking, and other things you want to do if you have learned the basics such as erecting the tent.

10

As a young person, you must camp with other people, including an experienced adult. When you are older, say sixteen or more, you will probably have learned enough camping skills to manage without an adult, but *never without a friend*. Accidents can happen on a camping trip, just as at home, and a companion is essential.

a word to adults

If your youngster is interested in camping, your principal role should be advisory. And that, as we all know, is most difficult for adults. We're too inclined to go ahead and do things. Don't, please!

Why? Well, part of the fun of camping for kids is for them to make selections and choices of their own. But relax, they'll need to ask your advice and discuss matters with you. For example, when a child is choosing a campground, there's a lot of information to be examined, and he or she will ask for your help.

11

It goes without saying that the choice of a campground area is of utmost importance, as is their choice of equipment. Go with them on the buying trip because some of the fanciest-looking equipment—lanterns and stoves and heaters—spell potential danger for youngsters.

Let your children begin with a simple outing and work toward longer, more challenging camping trips. You will help them gain skills which will offer relief from busy schedules in school and later on from work. One of the joys of camping for all ages is relaxation away from everyday life.

And be patient as they learn. It's a slow process. Children making decisions are like plants seeking the sun, a turn this way and a turn that way. You'll be able to participate, but it must be on their terms.

12

planning your trip

Planning is part of the fun. On rainy or cold nights, you may have time to look at camping catalogues, study maps, and plan your trip. Here are some of the things you should do. I am sure you will have other items to add to the list.

1. Choose your companions. They can be your family, friends and an experienced adult, or an organized group like the Scouts or the American Youth Hostel.*

*The American Youth Hostel is a non-profit association organized to encourage people of all ages to enjoy the out-of-doors and to travel simply and inexpensively. There are twenty-six Councils and many Hostel Clubs throughout the United States. Complete information may be obtained from the National Headquarters, 20 West Seventeenth Street, New York, New York 10011.

2. Decide where you will go and where you will stay. Information to help you is in Chapter 2. Will you hike or bike to the chosen area, take a train or a bus, be driven in a truck or station wagon?

3. Get maps—road maps from gasoline filling stations, camp maps from specific camps, topographic maps (if you want them) from the U. S. Geological Survey, Washington, D.C.

4. Choose equipment. Decide how you will pay for it. Perhaps you can borrow, rent, or receive some items as birthday gifts.

5. Select menus and write a grocery list. See page 62 for suggestions. Take into consider-

tion whether you will have a way to keep some foods such as eggs and lettuce fresh. Prepare meals several times in your back-yard or a nearby park that allows campfire cooking.

6. Practice hiking or bicycle riding. A day trip is an excellent way to get in training.

7. If you want to take your dog, check the campground regulations. Pets are subject to state laws, and some states require that dogs be kept on leash in camp and picnic grounds.

8. Prepare a time schedule for yourself. If you are going on a weekend trip, for example, estimate traveling time to and from the campground and plan each day's activities carefully.

chapter 2

where to go

types of campgrounds

Choose your campground carefully. Consider what you plan to do and how to get there.

There are basically five kinds of campgrounds in the United States with many services and facilities. They are: National Parks, National Forests, State Parks, County or Regional Parks, and Commercial Campgrounds. Let's start with National Parks.

national parks

You can watch prairie dogs in their village in Wind Cave National Park, Hot Springs, South Dakota;

take a boat ride through the subtropical forest and see alligators in Everglades National Park; or you can ride and fish in many National Parks.

There are more than 250 parks in the 50 states, Puerto Rico, and the Virgin Islands, with camping in 83 areas. Write to the Superintendent of Documents, U. S. Government Printing Office, Washington, D.C. 20402, for the booklet *Camping in the*

National Park System. Enclose $.25. Information is given on camping season, limit of stay, campground type, number of sites, fee, water and toilets, showers, laundry and stores, swimming, boating, fishing.

For additional information, write to the superintendent at the park in which you are interested. The address will be given in *Camping in the National Park System.*

RESERVATIONS

There are no reservations at National Parks. Campsites are on a first-come, first-served basis for individuals and small groups. However, organized groups like the Scouts can make reservations where there are special group camps.

FEES

An entrance fee is required for most areas, usually from $1.00 to $3.00 per day per site. It may be paid each day or by buying a $10 Golden Eagle Passport good in all Federal Recreation Areas for the year.

So-called "user" fees for hot water, electricity, etc., are in addition to entrance fees and are required at most areas where camping facilities are improved. User fees are paid as services are used.

There is no fee for backcountry camping.

RECREATION VEHICLES

Recreation vehicles are welcome in all parks and most campgrounds.

LENGTH OF STAY

The demand for campsites has made it necessary to limit the number of days a camper may keep a site. Details are available in *Camping in the National Park System*.

BACKCOUNTRY CAMPING

Camping is permitted in some areas away from established campgrounds and motor routes.

Such camping is only for older teen-agers, properly equipped and experienced, accompanied by an experienced adult. Discuss your plans and gear with the superintendent of the park or with a park ranger before proceeding with your plans, even if you are a seasoned camper.

19

FUEL

Everyone loves a campfire, but the shortage of wood in many areas (and the threat of air pollution in others) make a serious problem. You are encouraged to use charcoal in many National Parks for campfire cooking.

national forests

You can climb mountains at Signal Knob in the George Washington National Forest in Virginia, you can pick wild berries in the Gifford Pinchot National Forest in Washington, or you can hike, collect rocks, and sometimes swim and go boat riding in the National Forests run by the Forest Service under the Department of Agriculture.

There are 186 million acres of National Forest and National Grasslands. Write for the booklet *National Forest Vacations,* available for $.30 from the Superintendent of Documents, U. S. Government Printing Office, Washington, D.C. 20402. You can get detailed information and maps by writing to the Regional Forest in the area in which you are interested. The list is in the last chapter.

FACILITIES

National Forests are operated for conservation as well as enjoyment and, therefore, facilities are frequently different from those of the National Parks.

Although no two campgrounds are the same, they usually keep the forest atmosphere. You may find a cleared spot for a tent, a firegrate, table, and benches, or none of these things. Sometimes there are complete picnic areas located near the campgrounds.

RESERVATIONS

None are accepted. Campsites are filled on a first-come, first-served basis.

FEES

Entrance fees are required of all persons sixteen years of age or older. As in National Parks, special "user" fees are charged where such things as hot water, electricity, etc., are provided. If you do not use the facilities, you do not pay for them.

You may buy a Federal Recreation Area Entrance Permit costing $7.00 which may be used for a twelve-month period beginning April 1 of each year. The permit admits you to all National Forest charge areas, but not to a small number of recreation areas in the National Forests that are not included under the act. .

The permit may be purchased in person or by mail from Forest Service offices throughout the country, at Forest Service visitor centers, and from the Forest Service office, Room 4017, South Agriculture Building, U. S. Department of Agriculture, Washington, D.C. 20250. Make check or money order payable to the Treasurer of the United States.

TRAILERS

Small trailers may be used where parking space is large enough for car and trailer, but water, electrical, and sewage connections are not provided.

LENGTH OF STAY

Usually you may stay as long as you wish. A few popular areas limit visits to two weeks.

SEASON

The season runs from May 30 through Labor Day weekend, but in milder climates the season is longer and some are open year round.

CAMPFIRES

When you enter a National Forest, check with the ranger for permit requirements. Fires may usually be built at campgrounds, except in California. Cut fuelwood is sometimes available, sometimes not.

WATER

Most campgrounds have safe drinking water. Check detailed information from the Regional Forester's office.

SUPPLIES

You can seldom obtain supplies in the National Forest Area, only in nearby towns and, occasionally, from concessionaires.

23

state parks

State Parks offer a variety of activities. You can find beaver dams and excellent hiking trails in Stokes State Park in New Jersey; you can explore historic sites in Starved Rock State Park, Illinois. You can sometimes swim and fish.

The rules vary from state to state. It is, therefore, best to write for complete information in advance.

An entrance charge is usually made and sometimes a "user's fee."

Unless the State Parks and State Conservation Areas are near a metropolitan area, they are seldom as overcrowded for camping as many National Parks. The number of day visitors—fishing, swimming, hiking—may be large in number, but they leave the park at closing time.

Write to each state for information. You will find a listing in the last chapter.

county and regional parks

There are a few county and regional area campgrounds, but locating them is not easy without help from other campers, camp organizations, or residents.

If you know the county in which you want to camp, write to the County Clerk at the County Seat for information or the Chamber of Commerce in the nearest town.

commercial campgrounds

There are two types: private and franchised.

Most of them are planned as one-night stops on the way to somewhere else.

Private campgrounds are frequently inadequate although a number are pleasant and well run. Several directories list complete information. Woodall's *Trailering Parks and Campgrounds Directory* may be obtained at many camping and book stores or by writing to Woodall Publishing Co., 500 Hyacinth Place, Highland Park, Illinois 60035.

Franchise campgrounds are relatively new and offer facilities in attractive recreation areas as well as near-the-highway sites. KOA (Kamp Grounds Of America) have their headquarters in Montana. You can write to P. O. Box 1138, Billings, Montana 59103, for their directory.

KOA has a few ranch camps, complete with horseback riding, fishing, and other activities. They plan more.

An important feature of most franchise campgrounds, in addition to uniform quality, is that you can make a reservation.

tents

A tent keeps you dry and sheltered and protected from insects. Your tent should be a style that you can handle, practical for the kind of camping you plan, and as water repellent as possible. There are many types from which to choose.

Before you buy, it will be helpful to know where and how you will use your tent so that you can make a decision as to style and weight. It might be wise to rent a tent for your first trip to see how you like it.

Do not buy the cheapest tent. The price is low because many important features that make camp-

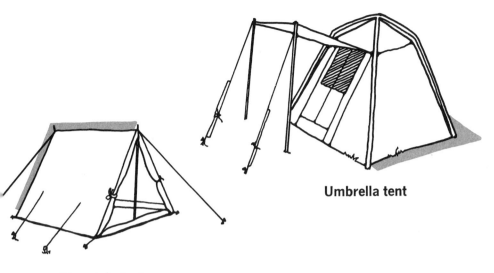

Umbrella tent

Mountain tent

Pop tent

Backpacker tent

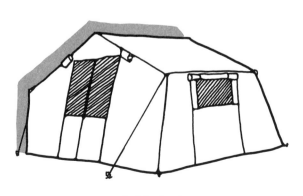

Cabin tent

ing pleasant are missing. A well-made tent lasts a long time, so if you cannot afford the best, buy a medium-priced one. Study the types of tents carefully in a camping catalogue, if you can, before you go into a store.

Among the considerations in buying a tent are:

WATER REPELLENCY

Find out everything there is to know about the fabric.

Water-repellent cotton tents with nylon or Dacron in the fabric are a good choice.

Nylon is an excellent material for tents, but a good water repellent (at this writing) has not been developed. You can combine a nylon tent with a sheet of plastic-coated nylon hung over the tent for protection. Nylon is not porous, as is cotton, and moisture gathers in the tent; and that is a disadvantage unless there is a great deal of ventilation.

VENTILATION

Ventilation is essential in tents to give you fresh air and to keep excess moisture from developing from your own breath and body.

Protection by mosquito netting at openings is necessary.

FLOOR

Unless you are backpacking and taking a trail tent tarp, which has no floor, you should make certain that the floor of your tent is sewn and reaches up the lower part of the walls.

29

STAKES, LINES, AND POLES

Tents usually come with stakes (also called pegs), guy lines (nylon line, cord, or light rope), and poles or frames. Be sure to take each piece of equipment and do not plan to cut poles at campsite. It is helpful to take additional lines or stakes if packing space is available because items are sometimes misplaced.

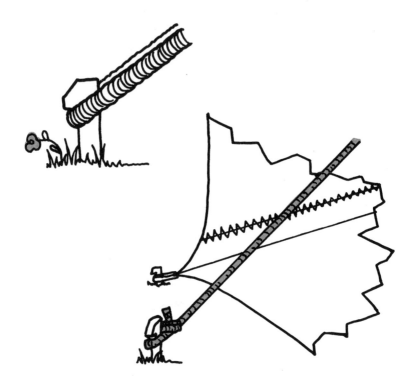

30

how to put up your tent

Some tents come with complete instructions and some do not. When you buy, ask for instructions. Perhaps the following procedure which we use would be helpful.

1. Remove rocks, pebbles, sticks from tent site.

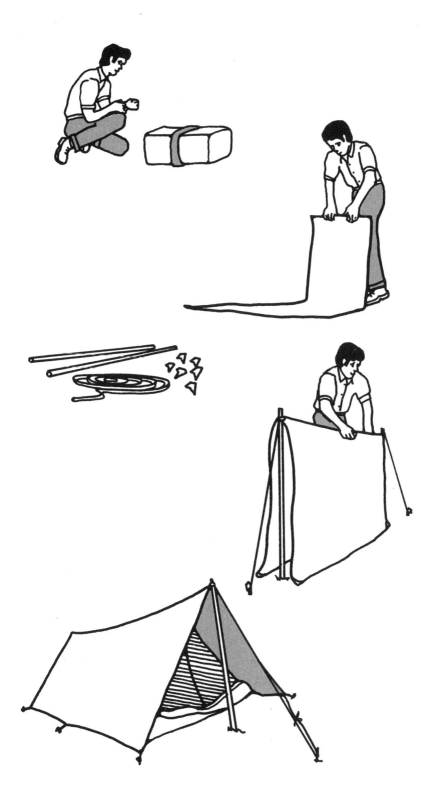

2. Spread tarp on ground.
3. Unwrap tent on tarp (to keep clean) and separate stakes, lines, and poles.

   Note: To keep track of stakes and guy lines, count number when removing from tent bag and recount when replacing after tent is taken down.

4. Close tent door and face tent on tarp away from campfire to keep smoke from entering opening. Tent should be at least ten to twenty feet away from fire for protection.
5. Drive stakes at four corners so that all are at right angles. Tie guy lines loosely.
6. Raise pole at tent peak, hammer stakes at additional spots, and fasten guy line with taut-line hitch. Raise other pole (if tent has two), tie down guy line, and stretch tent ridge between two poles.
7. Smooth floor.
8. Make certain all stakes are in place. Fasten all ropes and guy lines. Taut-line hitches are helpful because they can be easily tightened and loosened.
9. Tent should stand upright without sagging, sides and walls smooth but not too taut because rain shrinks canvas and lines.
10. After tent is erected, make certain that

opening is closed to keep out insects. Ventilation flaps should be open.

Note: The guy lines you purchase may have a metal taut-line hitch. If not, here are the instructions from the Scout Manual on tying one:

"Pass the rope through the eye or around the pole to which you want to attach it. Carry rope end around the standing part twice and through the loop thus formed. Then carry the rope end around once this time and pull taut. Finally adjust the knot."

SOME ADDITIONAL THOUGHTS
ON TENTS

Practice putting up your tent before your first trip. If you do not have a backyard, and no park is available, go through the necessary steps (without staking) in your room.

Keep your tent clean, inside and out, for all the reasons you know and because water repellency is more effective.

Keep your sleeping bag from rubbing against tent because contact may destroy the waterproofing.

34

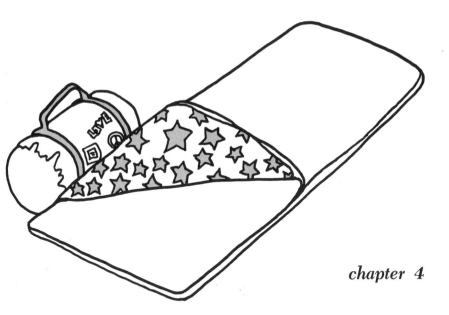

sleeping bags

A comfortable bed is important for a good night's sleep. The most convenient camp bed for you, I believe, is a sturdy water-repellent sleeping bag of the right weight and with a strong zipper. However, I will also tell you how to make a substitute.

35

Sleeping bags come in different shapes, sizes, and weights. You will find it easier to make a decision if you get a camping catalogue and study the differences. Some catalogues have easy-to-read charts which make comparison simpler.

Among the things you should look for:

FABRIC

Poplin—a lightweight cotton of good strength.

Duck—a heavy-duty cotton canvas of extra strength, preferred by many.

Nylon—a synthetic fabric, light and strong.

If possible, all fabrics should be water repellent; that is, treated to keep moisture out, but not direct rain. Waterproof material is unsatisfactory because body moisture cannot evaporate and one gets damp and uncomfortable.

FILLING

Polyester fiberfill fibers—a lightweight synthetic material which gives warmth and support.

36 *Down*—breast feathers of duck or goose which come in three weights. There is a difference of opinion as to whether it is too warm for ordinary camping.

Cotton—becomes cold and damp and lumps easily.

ZIPPER

Full length, separating.

HOOD

A sewn-on hood is helpful but not absolutely necessary.

AIR MATTRESS

Air mattresses are purchased separately. If you want to use one, the sleeping bag should have a pocket for it. You will need an air-mattress pump to blow up the mattress.

By the way, many campers prefer a polyester foam as a camp mattress under a sleeping bag. It is a good insulating material, lightweight, and easily folded. Kampamat is the brand name for one polyester foam mattress, and you may find others.

OTHER THINGS TO REMEMBER

Zippers should be handled carefully and slowly to prevent material catching.

If zippers are hard to work, or stick, apply zipper lubricant.

Sleeping bags should be laundered or sent to a professional dry cleaner, never to a self-service cleaner, because the fumes might not be adequately dissolved.

WHAT TO SLEEP IN

It is wise to sleep in pajamas, sweat shirt and pants, or long underwear. It is not wise to sleep in your regular clothes because the moisture given off by your body during the night is absorbed, and you will start the next day in damp clothing, which is not a good thing.

Wear an extra pair of socks to bed, if you need to, but change in the morning.

If your head gets cold, wear a skiing hat or a hood made from a large handkerchief.

Air your night clothes as well as your sleeping bag every day.

how to make a substitute for a sleeping bag

1. Use two wool blankets, not cotton. (Cotton holds dampness.)
2. Spread one wool blanket out flat.
3. Lay a second blanket so that it covers one half of the first blanket.
4. Fold first blanket to center.
5. Fold second blanket over it and pin at bottom and side with large safety pins.

6. Spread a waterproof poncho or ground cloth on ground under blanket bag to keep dampness from seeping through.

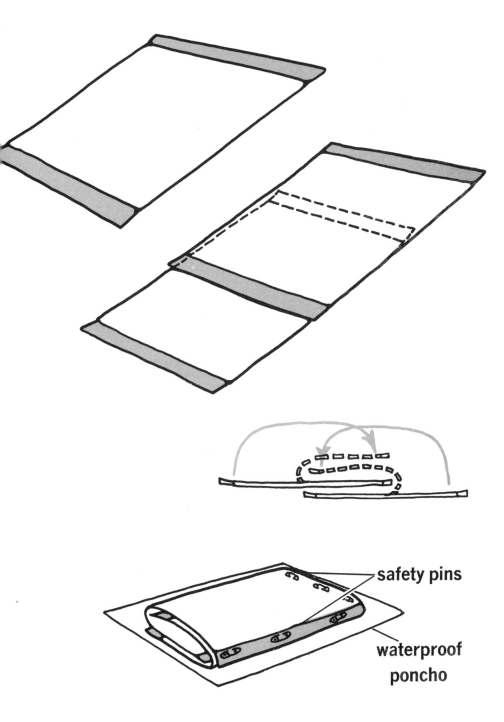

safety pins

waterproof poncho

camp life
setting up · while there
· breaking camp

40

Camp routine may seem a little difficult the first time, but you will be pleasantly surprised at how quickly you learn to do things in the right way.

When you arrive at the campground, register at the office and a site will be assigned to you, or you will be told to choose one. A list of regulations is available.

setting up

Two things to be done immediately on arrival at campsite: 1) set up tent; place sleeping bag, rain gear, insecticide, and flashlight inside. 2) Start fire and prepare first meal as soon as possible. The reason for the rush? You never, never know when it will rain.

Now that we have settled on your first jobs at campsite, let's look at the factors which will help you have a safe, comfortable, and happy time on your camping trip.

HERE'S WHAT YOU WANT
IN A CAMPSITE

1. A level piece of ground, although a slight slant is helpful to let rain water drain.
2. Ground for your tent that is reasonably clear of rocks, or that can be cleared, and soft enough so that tent stakes can be driven in.
3. Nearby water and wood supply.
4. Space for a garbage disposal and toilet area if such facilities are not part of campground.
5. Trees near enough to offer shade but far

41

enough so that you are not bothered by insects and waste matter from birds.

6. A site well above streams, rivers, lakes, or ponds which might overflow if heavy rains take place.

HERE'S WHAT YOU DO NOT WANT IN A SITE

1. Nearby overhanging cliffs or slopes from which landslides might start.
2. Trees with dead branches which might blow off during storms and land on your tent or site.

Note: If you have to take a less desirable location, check with park officials the following day and see if other sites are available.

42   MAKE CAMPSITE LIVABLE

Divide your campsite, even though small, into main areas of activity such as:

> cooking
> washing
> sleeping
> sanitary and garbage facilities, if not provided.

In the cooking area, which will probably be used for eating and relaxing also, choose a firesite first and then place:

storage hamper for foods

ice chest or cooler, if any, protected from sun

water supply

fuel supply

small work and eating table, or clear a level area and place a dropcloth or tarp there for that purpose.

If it is possible to do so, cover cooking area with a dropcloth or tarp fastened to poles or trees.

In the sleeping area, place your tent, as mentioned in the chapter on tents, at least ten to twenty feet away from the fire. Shake out your sleeping bag and place it along with other essential items in your tent.

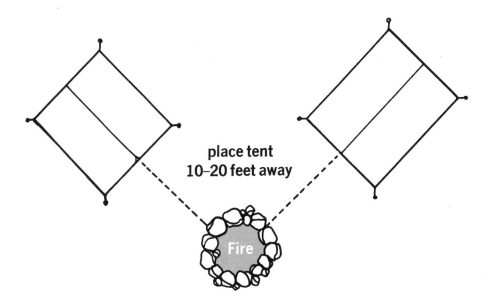

place tent
10–20 feet away

Fire

In the washing area, place a washbasin and soap along with a roll of paper towels for hand washing. String a line for cloth towels and wet clothes. If possible, hang a small mirror. Keep a can of wash water handy.

In the sanitary and garbage area, choose a place for disposal of garbage and a latrine area downhill and as far away as convenient to prevent unpleasant odors near camp and to keep from contaminating water supply by seepage.

Dig a pit deep enough for garbage.

camping area

garbage, soapy and greasy dishwater

fill to cover when leaving

Most campgrounds have some sanitary facilities, however primitive. If not, the simplest is a "cathole." Make a small hole in the ground by shoveling out some dirt. After use, fill in dirt.

By the way, nature has provided a way of decomposing in the top six to eight inches of soil. If campers co-operate, there will be no sanitation problems.

while there

CLEANUP AFTER MEALS

Each person should take turns cooking, but each should be responsible for cleaning his own eating utensils each time, or burning them if they are disposable. Cleanup should be done after every meal, and never left until later.

Gather left over or spilled pieces of food and dispose of them immediately. If liquid is spilled, rinse area thoroughly with water. Such actions are necessary to keep insects, birds, and animals from

45

Rinse area of spills

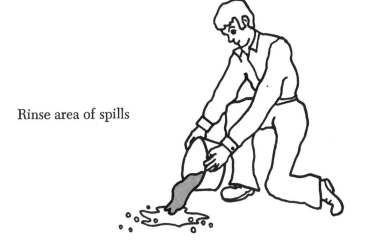

being attracted to your site. A camp should always be clean and pleasant smelling.

Water for washing dishes can be heated while you eat, or the kettle can be placed over the fire when it is first started before the flames settle down for cooking.

GARBAGE DISPOSAL

Burn everything except tin cans and aluminum pans. They should be packed out because they do not deteriorate. Rinse first and flatten if possible.

Dig a pit and put in burned garbage and excess grease from cooking. Cover with dirt and level.

For dishwater disposal, dig a hole and pour in dishwater. Cover with dirt. Never throw soapy or greasy dishwater in a stream or on the ground.

46   A FEW GOOD HABITS

These are suggestions which may be helpful. You'll have more to add because camping is a very personal affair.

At all times keep food containers closed and stored in air-tight hamper. Position food-hamper and cooler as far from sleeping area as possible in order to avoid attracting animals and insects.

Establish regular habits of cleanliness; very important when camping. When you first get up, wash your face, brush hair, etc. It makes life easier for you and those with whom you are traveling.

While your campfire is beginning (and before you have breakfast), remove sleeping clothes and sleeping bag from the tent (remember to reclose front flap) to air them.

The reason—during the night your body gives off moisture which is absorbed by your clothing and bedding.

The method—unzip sleeping bag or unfold blankets, and spread on dry ground, rocks, or over a heavy line or pole. Turn sleeping clothes inside out and do the same. Return to tent after they are dried; preferably before you begin morning activities.

Air out sleeping bag and sleeping clothes in morning

breaking camp

"Leave the campsite better than you found it."
Let that be your guide throughout camp breaking.

CARE OF TENT

Take your tent down after 10 A.M., if possible, to allow it to dry thoroughly after the night dampness.

Brush tent carefully to remove any loose dirt. Fold dry tent neatly and put in tent bag or tie with rope for easy handling. Never store a dirty tent for more than a day or two because it rots more quickly.

If you must leave earlier than midmorning, dry tent with paper towels as much as possible. A sponge is also helpful for cleaning.

PACKING

Pack the things you will need *last* at the *bottom* of your pack and the things you will need *first* at the *top*. For example, your poncho, rain hat, and sweater should always be at the top of your pack.

Pack in the same way each time so that you will know where items are.

CLEANING

Pick up litter and sweep campsite before you leave. A small whisk broom is useful and not difficult to pack.

Make certain all garbage is disposed of, as described in this chapter. Fill in any pits or holes.

SAFETY

Be sure that all fires are out and firesite covered with water or sand.

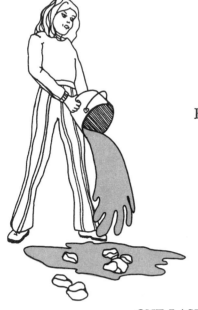

Be Sure Fire Is Definitely Out

ONE LAST LOOK

Go back systematically over every foot of camp space to look for forgotten items.

camp cooking · part 1

Before we can talk about what to cook, we must talk about the way in which we will cook—over an open fire or on a small portable stove. Ask park or campground officials for rules on fire building.

50

over an open fire

Start fire about one and a half hours before cooking. Flames need time to settle down and give steady heat. There is, however, usually enough heat at the beginning to boil water for a cup of tea, or bouillon, or instant cereal.

There are several different types of fires to choose from. Remember that cooking fires should be built small and safe.

1. **Hunter's or trapper's fire**
    Place two logs, flatter side up, side by side in something like a V shape, close together at one end, more open at the other, facing into the wind.

    Pots and teakettles are placed upon the two logs.

Hunter's or Trapper's Fire

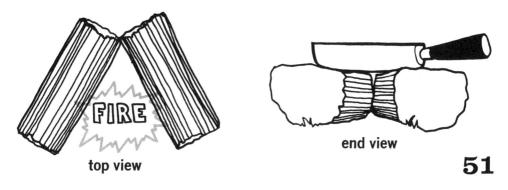

top view

end view

51

2. **Rock fire**
    Place a ring of rocks in a small circle piled high enough so that the pots need not be too close to the flames.

    You can then place a flat rock on top of the

circle on which to rest pots, or the circle can be small enough so that pots are placed directly over flame.

Rock Fire

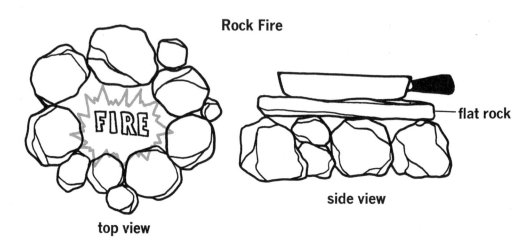

flat rock

side view

top view

3. **Trench fire**

A trench fire should be used only where there are few trees and little else growing.

Dig a narrow trench about six inches deep, slanting up from deepest part to ground level, facing into the wind.

52

Width should be planned so that cooking utensils rest on the ground and over the fire.

Trench Fire

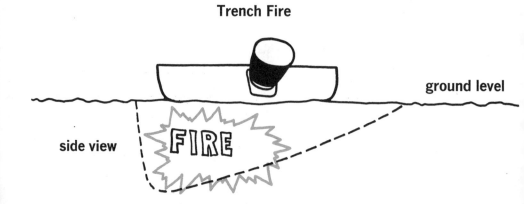

ground level

side view

Before we build a fire, here are things
to remember:

1. Clear away grass, leaves, twigs, etc., within ten feet of fire.

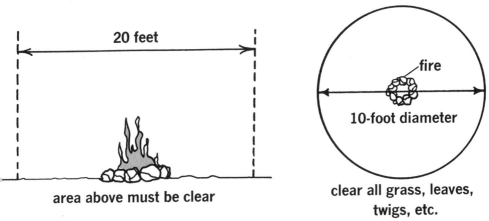

area above must be clear

clear all grass, leaves, twigs, etc.

2. Build fire on rocks, sand, or dirt.
3. Build away from overhanging tree branches or dead trees.
4. If campfire site has been used before, remove old material.
5. Have buckets of water or sand nearby for emergencies. To put out a fire, sprinkle continuously with small amount of water, sand, or dirt until fire is out. Soak ground around fire. When fire is definitely out, cover with dirt.
6. Gather wood all at once, if possible, and sort into three piles; twigs (called tinder), kindling, larger pieces. Saw large pieces into right length as soon as possible. Cover wood to protect from possible rain.

53

building a fire

1. *Tinder*—dried leaves, pine needles, small twigs, or shredded paper.
2. *Kindling*—small split pieces of wood which will help ignite large pieces.
3. *Firewood*—almost any dry wood will do. Branches of dried evergreens, however, are sometimes too smoky and burn too fast.
4. *Dry matches.*

And here's what you do:

54 Arrange a small amount of tinder at center of fireplace. Make a small tepee of kindling around tinder, leaving space between pieces of wood to permit air to circulate.

Note: Some seasoned campers like to place a kettle of water in place over fire before lighting.

Light and, when fire is burning well, add more kindling. Then place larger pieces of wood, one at at a time, until fire is the size you have planned.

If you have been unable to learn in advance if wood is available, take along sufficient charcoal or briquettes. Plan ahead for windy or rainy days, when fire making is more difficult, by taking a safe chemical such as "Fire Starter" to help get fire going."Instant Self Starting Brix Jumbo Pack" is a convenient self-starting charcoal.

GRILLS

There are several types of lightweight grills to be placed over charcoal or wood fires which make cooking somewhat easier, but add weight to your pack. Among them are a backpack camp grill of lightweight steel, 8″ x 12″, which folds up and one 15½″ x 5″ with a cover. The protection of a cover is helpful in packing.

cooking on a portable stove

The Sterno stove is the only one I would recommend for youngsters. The two-burner folding stove weighs only two pounds, and folds flat when not in use. From the standpoint of packing, it is probably better to take 2 one-burner Sterno stoves.

The heat comes from canned Sterno, which is a solid, non-melting portable fuel, non-explosive and odorless. It is easy to light, burns steadily, and the flame can be put out and relit as needed until the can is emptied. There are two sizes.

You can buy a windscreen for the Sterno stove which makes it more efficient in bad weather.

The following two stoves are NOT TO BE USED BY CHILDREN, but they are included in this book for a practical reason. Your adult companion, if an experienced camper, will find the stoves helpful if a spell of bad weather makes a campfire impossible.

1. **SVEA 123 Gasoline Camp Stove**
    Lightweight (18 ounces), small (5″ x 3¾″), when closed is about the size of a can of soup, has windshield, burns 45 minutes on ⅓ pint gasoline.
    Safety valve in filler cap.
    Aluminum cover can be cooking pot.

Fuel should be carried in safe container such as red anodized one-quart or one-pint aluminum bottle, with shackled screw cap with gasoline-proof gasket, or larger galvanized gas cans.

2. **Optimus Camping Stove**
Lightweight (1 pound 9 ounces), small (5″ x 5″ x 3″), compact, windproof, and efficient in any weather.

Burns ordinary gasoline which may be carried as described above.

Note: Plan your fuel supply carefully or check in advance to be certain that supplies are available at or near your campsite.

camp cooking · part 2

pots and pans

Choose cooking pots and pans carefully, preferably heavy-duty aluminum with Teflon which provides even cooking while using little or no grease in frying.

Try to find a simple, nested cooking set composed of a frying pan, small and large saucepans (all with covers). If you can not find the right combination, buy them separately. Some sets come with a bag for carrying; if not, buy one. Make certain that individual utensils nest snugly into each other. You will also need a camp kettle for heating water, the kind we call a teakettle at home.

A heavy-duty griddle with Teflon is convenient for cooking if you are not carrying supplies a long distance.

A disposable heavy-aluminum-foil 9-inch frying pan is generally available. It may be reused.

Disposable aluminum cake and pie pans can be used in a variety of ways for camp cooking. (Remember, however, that all aluminum must be packed out.)

eating accessories

Use paper, plastic-coated, or plastic disposable plates, cups, bowls, knives, forks, and spoons.

You may think it is expensive to buy a sufficient supply, but they make work lighter and, more importantly, they are safer. If dishes are not properly rinsed of soapsuds, diarrhea can result. Water is precious in camp and rinsing dishes carefully, as at home, is difficult. Many seasoned campers do not use soap at all but wash dishes in hot water to remove grease.

You will find a list of suggested tools and accessories later on.

refrigeration

An ice chest or hamper is not absolutely essential, but it makes storage of perishable items more convenient. A number of different sizes and models are available. You do not need a very large one.

Stock the chest with ice before leaving on your trip, if practical. You might also add several cans of chemical ice available through hardware stores as well as camping stores. Chemical ice has the advantage of reuse; simply freeze again.

If possible, pack food in the bottom of the cooler with ice on top so that cold penetrates downward.

An insulated bag, chilled in advance, is helpful in keeping fruits and vegetables fresh; and might continue to be used at the campsite with a can of chemical ice inserted. Take care that items are not close enough to ice to freeze.

Ice is usually available near or at campgrounds. In the Midwest and West, it is often sold at filling stations.

camp cooking · part 3

planning meals

There's a very simple reason for planning all meals in advance. You are free of worry about what you're going to eat. And it's really not difficult if you keep the following in mind:

1. Plan Menus For All Meals

If the menus on the following pages appeal to you, then step #1 is almost done for you. Substitutions because of personal likes can easily be made.

2. Buy Groceries Before You Leave

Plan menus so that meals can be prepared at camp completely from groceries purchased before leaving; or, at the most, by buying a few supplies, such as eggs, midweek, if you have learned that supplies are available.

3. Hints for Packing

To cut down breakage:

Buy foods in plastic containers when possible.

Transfer foods in glass (such as barbecue sauce) to plastic jars with tight lids.

To cut down weight:

Buy packaged items rather than canned when possible.

Transfer dry foods, such as pancake mix, to heavyweight nylon or plastic bags with zip-lock seal or well-tied. (Dental floss is excellent for tying.)

Small or large sizes:

Whether you buy two small cans of food, or one large can, will depend upon how you are packing and distributing grocery supplies.

4. Emergency Food

Camping catalogues and stores have a number of "emergency" foods under different brand names. It is a sound idea for each camper to carry one or more in his pack. Among such items are the "Pemmican Woodsman Emergency Kit" which supplies enough food energy for twenty-four hours, several meats like "Beef Jerky," and a highly nutritional "Tropical Chocolate Bar" which won't melt.

5. A Word About Some Foods in the Menus

About non-fat dry milk . . . it is pleasant to taste. If you add chocolate-flavored powder, as everyone seems to, you can scarcely recognize any difference from whole milk. By preparing the amount needed for each meal, refrigeration is not necessary. Keep package airtight for best flavor.

About eggs . . . if refrigerated they will, of course, keep their freshness for several weeks. If no cooler is used at campsite, here's what you do: Before leaving, chill eggs thoroughly, wrap in insulating material such as heavy-duty aluminum foil; pack in insulated bag with package of chemical ice. Under these conditions eggs should remain fresh in camp for two or three days and can be used for breakfast the first morning and French toast the second. At normal summer temperature eggs, without such protection, will remain fresh for eight to twelve hours. Powdered eggs are available through camping-supply stores and catalogues. They may be used cooked in any form in which fresh eggs are used. There is, I feel, an unjustified prejudice against cooking with powdered eggs. Keep package airtight.

64

About margarine . . . it is preferable to butter because it keeps its fresh taste longer.

About toast . . . many find that toasting is a waste of time. Once you become accustomed to untoasted bread at breakfast, toast becomes unimportant on a camping trip. Or you could take along Melba or another prepared toast.

About cereals . . . your concern, when camping, should be with those which are high in protein. You may know of other brands which are equally satisfactory.

About smoked ham . . . if taken to campground in cooled insulated bag, should maintain freshness until second day.

About optional items . . . there are only a few listed for emergency or personal preference.

suggested menus and grocery list for four people for seven days

first day

Breakfast

Orange Drink
Cereal with Bananas or Raisins
Boiled Eggs
Whole Wheat or Rye Bread   Margarine
    Jelly
Cocoa   Milk

Lunch

Cheese, Lettuce, and Tomato Sandwiches
Dill Pickles
Raisins and Nuts
Milk   Hot Bouillon

Evening Meal

Barbecued Beef on Bun *
Peas   Potatoes
Chocolate Pudding
Milk

Snacks

Cookies and Camper's Punch *

second day

Breakfast

Grapefruit and Orange Juice
Cereal
French Toast with Syrup or Jelly
Cocoa   Milk

An * means the recipe or a suggestion on cooking is given later on.

Lunch

Peanut Butter and Jelly Sandwiches
Cucumber Slices and Celery Sticks
Oranges
Milk   Hot Bouillon

Evening Meal

Grilled Ham Slice
Sweet Potatoes   Green Pepper Slices
Vanilla Pudding
Milk

Snacks

Graham Crackers and High-Protein Drink*

third day

Breakfast

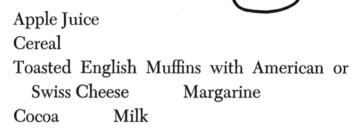

Apple Juice
Cereal
Toasted English Muffins with American or
    Swiss Cheese   Margarine
Cocoa   Milk

Lunch

High-Protein Sandwiches
Apples or Applesauce
Milk   Fruit Drink

Evening Meal

Spaghetti and Meat Balls
Carrot and Cabbage Slaw
Rye Bread   Butter
Bananas with Chocolate Sauce and Nuts
Milk

Snacks

Toasted Marshmallows and Sugar-Sweetened
    Grape Drink

fourth day

Breakfast

Honey-flavored Prunes (Sweeten with
    honey instead of sugar.)
Cereal
French Toast with Syrup or Jelly
Cocoa   Milk

Lunch

Tuna Fish Sandwiches on Rye Bread
Sliced Tomatoes and Lettuce
Cookies   Milk

Evening Meal

Barbecued Spanish Rice with Meat*
Green Beans
Cracked Wheat Bread
Oranges or Canned Mandarin Oranges

Snacks

Buttered Popcorn and High-Protein Drink*

70   fifth day

Breakfast

Orange Juice
Cereal
Pancakes with Syrup and Margarine
Cocoa   Milk

Lunch

Deviled Ham-Peanut Butter Sandwiches on
   Rye Bread
Sliced Tomatoes
Fruit Cocktail
Milk   Tea

Evening Meal

Pork and Beans with Canned Meat*
Salad with Lettuce, Tomatoes, and Other
   Available Fresh Vegetables
Grilled Pineapple Cubes
Caramel Pudding*
Milk

71

Snacks

Cookies and Camper's Punch*

sixth day

Breakfast

>   Apple Juice
>   Cereal
>   Canned Luncheon Meat Grilled
>   Wholewheat or Rye Bread   Margarine
>   Jelly
>   Cocoa   Milk

Lunch

>   Peanut Butter-Fruit Sandwiches on White*
>   Carrot Sticks and Green Pepper Slices
>   Cookies
>   Milk   Hot Bouillon

Evening Meal

>   Glazed Meat Cubes*
>   Green Beans
>   Applesauce Pudding*
>   Milk

Snacks

>   Graham Crackers and Fruit Punch

seventh day

Breakfast

Apricot Nectar
Cereal
Pancakes with Syrup or Jelly
Cocoa   Milk

Lunch

Beef Sandwiches with Lettuce and Tomato*
Apples or Canned Applesauce
Milk   Hot Bouillon

Evening Meal

Chicken with Rice
Peas   Sliced Tomatoes
Butterscotch Pudding
Milk

73

Snacks

Chocolate-Peanut Fondue* and Camper's
Punch*

BARBECUED BEEF ON BUN

⅔ cup beef gravy
⅓ cup barbecue sauce, such as Open Pit,
    any flavor
8 ounces cooked roast beef,
    sliced or diced (about 2 cups)
4 hamburger buns, toasted

Combine beef gravy and barbecue sauce in sauce-pan. Heat until bubbly. Add meat and continue cooking over fire until meat is thoroughly heated. Serve on toasted buns.

Makes 4 servings.

BARBECUED SPANISH RICE WITH MEAT

74

1 package (6 ounces) Minute Spanish Rice Mix
1 can (1 pound) tomatoes
1 cup water
2 tablespoons margarine
1 can (12 ounces) Pork and Beef Luncheon Meat

Measure two 18-inch square sheets of heavy-duty aluminum foil. Place on top of one another in medium-size bowl or saucepan. Press down to form a pouch. Combine rice, contents of seasoning packet, tomatoes, meat cut in cubes, water, and margarine in pouch. Fold foil to seal tightly and remove pouch from bowl.

Place on grill over hot coals. Cook 10 minutes; turn pouch over. Continue cooking about 10 minutes longer. Remove from grill. Open foil and fluff rice.

Makes about 6 servings.

CAMPER'S PUNCH

> 1 envelope sugar-sweetened Kool-Aid
>   orange soft drink mix
> 2 cups pineapple juice
> ¼ cup lemon juice (fresh or bottled)
> 1 quart cold water

75

Combine all ingredients. Stir until instant soft drink mix is dissolved.

Makes almost 2 quarts or 20 servings.

Note: Regular or sugar-sweetened Kool-Aid instant soft drink mix should be prepared in a non-metal or stainless steel container.

CHICKEN RICE

1 package (7 ounces) Minute Rice Mix
2 cups water
2 tablespoons margarine
2 cans boned chicken

Measure two 18-inch square sheets of heavy-duty aluminum foil. Place on top of one another in medium-size bowl or saucepan; press down to form a pouch. Combine contents of package, water, margarine, and chicken in pouch. Fold foil to seal tightly and remove from bowl.

Place on grill over hot coals. Cook 10 minutes; turn pouch over. Continue cooking about 10 minutes longer. Remove from grill. Open foil and fluff rice.

Makes about 4 cups or 6 servings.

CARAMEL PUDDING

2 small cans, or 1 large can, condensed milk

Fill saucepan half-full of water (preferably hot) and bring to a boil.

Place unopened cans, or can, in water completely covered. Position saucepan on fire so that water continues to simmer, not boil, for approximately one and a half hours.

Milk will caramelize into a pudding that is similar to a popular Mexican dessert.

This recipe should be prepared around the campfire at night in preparation for the next day.

APPLESAUCE PUDDING

1 package vanilla-flavor instant pudding
1½ cups milk
½ cup applesauce

Prepare pudding according to directions using 1½ cups milk, and stir in applesauce.

PORK AND BEANS WITH CANNED MEAT

The meat can be our familiar pork and beef luncheon meat, or vienna frankfurters, or shredded dried beef.

BEEF SANDWICHES

Although dried beef tends to be salty, if you add lettuce and tomato, you have a satisfactory sandwich. Canned roast beef is available in some stores, and you might want to experiment with both to see which you prefer.

CHOCOLATE-PEANUT FONDUE

¼ cup butter or margarine
4 squares (4 ounces) unsweetened chocolate
2 cups sugar
1 cup water
½ cup peanut butter
1 teaspoon vanilla
Marshmallows

78 Combine all ingredients in small saucepan (except marshmallows) and stir over low fire until melted and smooth. Spear marshmallows on clean twigs and dunk into fondue.

This recipe can be prepared at home in advance. Pour into heavy-duty transparent plastic or nylon bag. Seal well. At campsite, pour into small saucepan and heat over fire while stirring.

Makes 2½ cups.

DEVILED HAM-PEANUT BUTTER SANDWICH FILLING

1 (2¼ ounces) can deviled ham
Equal amount of peanut butter
1 tablespoon lemon juice (fresh or bottled)

Empty can of deviled ham into small bowl. Use can to measure peanut butter. Add to ham along with lemon juice. Stir thoroughly.

Yield: ⅔ cup, or filling for 4 sandwiches.

FRUIT PUNCH

1 envelope sugar-sweetened Kool-Aid
    soft drink mix, any flavor
1 cup unsweetened pineapple juice
1 quart cold water

Combine all ingredients, stirring until soft drink mix is dissolved.

Makes about 5 cups or 10 servings.

Note: sugar-sweetened Kool-Aid soft drink mix should be prepared in a non-metal or stainless steel container.

GLAZED MEAT CUBES

1 can (12 ounces) pork and beef luncheon meat
1 can (13½ ounces) pineapple chunks
   (optional)
maple-blended syrup

Cut luncheon meat into 24 cubes. Drain pineapple chunks. Alternately place meat cubes and pineapple on skewers. Dribble with syrup.

Can be placed in shallow pan over fire for about 15 minutes, or until thoroughly heated; or skewers placed directly over low flame and turned until golden brown.

Makes 4 servings.

HIGH-PROTEIN SANDWICH SPREAD

1 cup peanut butter
½ cup honey
½ cup crumbled crisp bacon or ¼ cup
   packaged bacon-flavored bits
½ cup wheat germ
1 cup well-drained crushed pineapple

Combine all ingredients and blend well. If necessary add juice of canned pineapple until spread is the right consistency. Pack mixture into a plastic jar or container and seal well.

This can be prepared in advance, leaving out fruit, and packed into heavy-duty plastic or nylon bag. Just before preparing sandwiches, add well-drained crushed pineapple to mixture, adding some juice if necessary for right spreading consistency.

HIGH-PROTEIN DRINK

1 package powdered milk
4 cups water
4 tablespoons Tang or 1 package Kool-Aid

Mix ingredients together until thoroughly dissolved. Chill if possible.

PEANUT BUTTER-FRUIT SANDWICH 81

peanut butter
2 bananas
2 apples

Spread peanut butter on both slices. Thinly slice half a banana and half of a peeled apple. Layer fruit between peanut-buttered slices of white bread.

list of groceries for seven days' camping

canned vegetables

2 cans Peas #1 (10½ oz.)
2 cans Green Beans #2 (1 lb., 4 oz.)
4 cans White Potatoes (8 oz. each) (optional as a substitute)
1 can Sweet Potatoes #1 (10½ oz.)
1 can Pork and Beans (2 lbs.)
2 small cans Condensed Milk (or 1 large)
1 can Tomatoes #2 (1 lb.)
  Fruits and Juices

canned fruits and juices

1 can Apricot Nectar #2 (1 lb., 4 oz.)
1 can Grapefruit and Orange Juice (1 qt., 12 oz.)
1 can Orange Juice (1 qt., 12 oz.)
3 cans Pineapple Juice #2 (1 pt., 2 fl. oz.)
2 packages (6 cans) Apple Juice or two 1-quart cans
1 can Apricots #303 (16 oz.) (optional as a substitute)

2 cans Mandarin Orange Segments (11 oz.) (optional as a substitute)

2 cans Pineapple Cubes #2 (13½ oz.)

1 can Fruit Cocktail #303 (1 lb.)

1 can Peaches #1 (10½ oz.) (optional as a substitute)

1 can Applesauce #2 (1 lb., 4 oz.)

canned meats, fish, chicken

2 cans Boned Chicken (5 oz.)

1 can Deviled Ham (2½ oz.)

2 cans Pork and Beef Luncheon Meat (12 oz.)

2 cans Spaghetti and Meat Balls (15½ oz.)

2 cans Tuna Fish (7 oz.)

other

3 large boxes Dry Non-Fat Milk (each box contains 10 packets, one packet makes 1 quart milk)

2 small cans, or 1 large, Condensed Milk
Several packages Instant Sweetened Tea Mix

1 container Beef Bouillon cubes or packets

1 container Chicken Bouillon cubes or packets

4 packages high-protein cereal such as Crunchy Granola, Familia, Quick Cooking Oatmeal, Post's Fortified Oat Flakes, or Kellogg's Concentrate

1 package Wheat Germ (which some use as a dry cereal)

1 can or bottle Pancake Syrup

1 jar Honey

1 2-pound box Granulated Sugar (or 2 1-pound boxes)
small packages Salt and Pepper

1 package Bacon-Flavored Bits

1 jar Dill Pickles

1 package or 1 can Dry Beef Gravy

1 small bottle Vegetable Oil

1 half-pint jar Mayonnaise
small jars Mustard, Ketchup, Relish, and Barbecue Sauce
such as Open Pit

1 package Prunes (1 pound)

2 packages Raisins (6 or 8 individual packets to package or
2 1-pound boxes)

1 can shelled Walnuts

1 large jar Powdered Orange Drink such as Tang

6 packages Kool-Aid (different flavors, grape, cherry, orange,
etc.)

1 large box Instant Cocoa mix

1 jar Chocolate-flavored Syrup

1 large jar Peanut Butter #300 (15 oz.)

1 jar Grape Jelly (12 oz.)

2 boxes Salted Peanuts (8 packets to box)

1 can Pop Corn

1 large package Marshmallows

1 bar Unsweetened Chocolate Squares

1 package Minute Rice

1 package Minute Spanish Rice

3 packages Instant Pudding mix

3 boxes Cookies

1 box Graham Crackers

1 small box Pancake Mix (1 lb.)

bread

2 loaves Enriched White
2 loaves Whole or Cracked Wheat
1 loaf Rye
1 package Hamburger Buns (4 to package)
1 package English Muffins (16 to package)
2 boxes Saltine Crackers

meats

2 packages Dried Beef (in sealed plastic bag)
  Sliced cooked Roast Beef (1½ to 2 lbs.)
  Ham Slice, 2" thick, precooked (about 2 lbs.)
1 or 2 cans Imported Bacon to have on hand for emergencies

85

dairy

2 dozen Eggs
1 pound Margarine
1 package Processed American-type Cheese (8 slices)
1 package Swiss Cheese (8 slices)

fresh

8 Bananas, 4 Oranges, 4 Apples
2 large heads Lettuce (or 4 small)
10 Tomatoes
4 Cucumbers
1 bunch Celery
2 Green Peppers
3 bunches Carrots
1 head of Cabbage
1 Lemon

86

backpacking

If you and your family, or you and your friends, have become experienced trustworthy campers, and are in good physical condition, then backpacking can be an extraordinary adventure. Such camping does not, however, appeal to everyone. The word "backpacking," as we are using it, means going into "back country," undeveloped areas that are mostly in National Forests, National Parks, Wildlife Refuges, and Ranges. (The word is also used by campers to refer to a style of hiking which might be to any campground, not necessarily wilderness.)

87

Backpacking, let me emphasize, calls for the best that you can give to camping—wise planning, experience, nutritious and carefully selected food, and proper equipment.

Wise planning means that, in addition to the suggestions given in previous chapters, you must learn in detail about the areas you have selected, special equipment that might be required, and the best time to make the trip. For example, mountain trips should probably be taken from mid-July to mid-September. A desert trip, or a southern wilderness trip, might call for late winter and early spring. The forest ranger or park superintendent will advise you.

Planning means choosing the best way to travel: hiking, riding horseback, canoeing, or river floating. I suggest you choose a pack-trip outfitter who will have guide services. He will provide food, tents, and other equipment, and you will bring your own sleeping bag and personal belongings.

Seasoned experience, which is imperative, commonly comes through camping many times in different places, in different ways. Experience is as important for adults as for children.

If your food is not supplied by a pack-trip outfitter, read the suggested menus in Chapter 7 and see if you can substitute powdered and freeze-dried foods. You will need to select carefully to stay within the minimum amount. Keep in mind that each person needs 1½ pounds of food per day.

Although I have given you a list of items you need for camping, the backpacking trip calls for special care and you will find helpful information prepared by the Wilderness Society, 729 Fifteenth Street, N.W., Washington, D.C. 20005. Here's what they say in *Off on the Right Foot: A Guide to Proper Wilderness Use.*

things you'll need –
the backpacking trip

"Pack (packboard, framework, or rucksack), tent or tarp, sleeping bag and air mattress, one-burner lightweight gasoline stove, cooking utensils, dishes (plates, cups, and cutlery), and food (at least 1½ pounds a day per person).

"Clothing (2 pairs of slacks or jeans, at least 2 long-sleeved cotton shirts, wool shirt, sweater, parka, inner and outer wool socks, warm sleeping suit, underwear, and camp shoes), plastic raincoat or poncho, handkerchiefs, flashlight, first-aid kit,

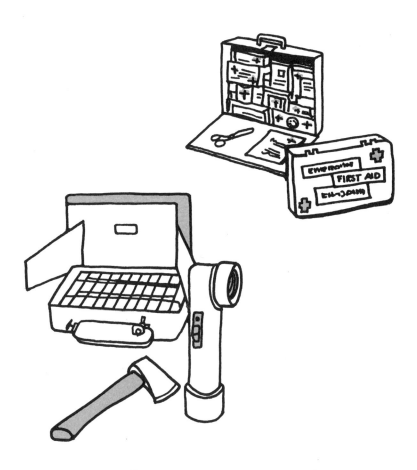

mosquito repellent, compass, maps and map case, suntan and skin lotion, dark glasses, rope (nylon cord), toilet tissue, knife, ax or hatchet, fishing tackle with rod in metal case, small pliers, safety matches, chapped-lip medication, soap and towel, needle and thread, and safety pins.

"Total weight of the pack should be limited to 30 pounds for women, 40 pounds for men.

"Footwear with eyelets and lacing has proved best for hiking. Most backpackers prefer 7- to 10-inch laced boots with rubber, synthetic, or cord soles. Footwear should be broken in and fit comfortably over two pairs of socks, one light and one heavy. Take extra laces."

camping by the sea

Along with the joy of ocean and sun, the seashore offers gifts of rocks and seashells. Sometimes beach plums and bayberries grow just beyond the tide-line. If the coast is rocky, you may find tidal pools where many kinds of sea life grow. Water is trapped when the tides go out and fiddler crabs, whelks, seaweed, starfish, and other lovely things may be seen.

93

Camping by seashore parks like Padre Island National Seashore in Corpus Christi, Texas, or Assateague Island National Seashore, Berlin, Maryland, means following the advice already given with a few additional suggestions. That is why I have placed this information in a separate chapter for you.

You will find names and information on national and state seashore camping in the publications listed in Chapter 14. Many may be crowded at the height of the season, and you will want to remember that in your planning.

When you secure a campsite, place your camp well above the highest tidemark. Tide charts, which will be available from the park superintendent, will list high and low tides.

To pitch your tent in sand, extra-long stakes are helpful. Some seasoned campers use rocks or heavy pieces of driftwood tied to the guy lines and buried deep in the sand.

Keep your tent fastened tightly at all times to prevent sand from sifting inside. An additional plastic sheeting or tarp will provide needed shade and help protect your tent from wind and sand.

There is, as you have noticed, a list of items needed for general camping. You will want most of them, but sunglasses, a hat, long-sleeved shirt, and suntan lotion are absolute necessities for the beach.

Observe the rules of the park, as you always do, and you will find fun and treasures of unusual seashells, lovely pieces of driftwood, and perhaps excellent fish to eat.

camping in canada

Canada is big and wild and also civilized enough to offer you almost any experience in camping. If you can make arrangements yourself or if you can join a Youth Hostel trip, you will have a wide choice of lakes and streams, quiet beaches, deep woods and wilderness.

95

From the Pacific, with sea lions off the Pacific Rim National Park, to the Atlantic, with the world's highest tides in Fundy National Park, there are twenty-four National and thirty-three Historic parks. Each of the ten provinces has its own parks, known as provincial parks. Along the Trans-Canada Highway, approximately 5,000 miles long, there is a campground almost every 100 miles and a picnic ground every 50. There are also many privately operated campgrounds.

federal government operated campgrounds

FEES

Daily fees are $1.50 for a site; $2.00 for a site with electricity; and $2.50 for a site with water, electricity, and sewer connections.

The National Parks motor vehicle fee is $2.00 for an annual license. Some provinces have additional motor vehicle fees and some do not. The price can be different from province to province.

Daily fees at provincial park campgrounds are from $1.00 to $4.00.

CAMPSITES

Campsites are on a first-come, first-served basis and no reservations can be made. Length of stay is usually two weeks.

PETS

Leashed dogs and other pets kept under control are admitted to National Parks and some provincial campgrounds.

GROUP CAMPING

Group tenting sites are available in some parks for organized groups. Write for information to the park superintendent.

OTHER INFORMATION

Camping outside established campgrounds is not allowed unless permission is obtained from the park warden. Camping in picnic areas or along the highway and roads is not permitted.

Nearly all campgrounds offer free firewood. Wood fires are permitted only in grills and fireplaces especially made for this purpose.

border crossing between the united states and canada

To cross the border from the United States to Canada, American citizens need a birth or baptismal certificate, or voter's card and draft card if you are over eighteen years old. You do not need a passport or visa.

If your group is being taken by car, the driver should have Motor Vehicle Registration forms. If the car is not his own, he must have either a rental contract or a letter of permission from the owner. International and U.S.A. state drivers' licenses may be used.

Young people under eighteen need a letter from either parent giving permission to travel.

98

FISHING EQUIPMENT

A description of fishing equipment should be given to customs officers. Each province has its own regulations, and you must follow them. Write for fishing regulations and the proper non-resident licenses.

YOUR DOG

You need the dog's license and a veterinarian's signed certificate describing the dog and stating that he has been vaccinated against rabies during the last year.

COMING BACK

You must stop at the border for inspection by U. S. Immigration authorities in order to re-enter.

travel service

Here is a listing of excellent booklets for which you may write directly to the Canadian Government Travel Bureau, Ottawa, Canada, or to their offices in the United States. All are free except *Family Camping.* Canadian and American postage rates are the same. Canadians may obtain information directly from the Canadian Government Travel Bureau, Ottawa, Ontario, KIA OH 6, or from their provincial government.

Canada National Parks.
Canada, National and Historic Parks.

Canada Campgrounds, tenting, trailer and picnic sites along the trans-Canada Highway.
So You're Going to Canada.
Family Camping ($.75).

The Canadian Government Travel Bureau provides a free travel service which you can obtain either by writing them in Ottawa, or contacting the office nearest you.

Boston, Massachusetts 02199
263 Plaza
The Prudential Center

Buffalo, New York 14202
1417 Main Place

Chicago, Illinois 60602
100 North La Salle Street

Cincinnati, Ohio 45202
Room 1010
Enquirer Building
617 Vine Street

Cleveland, Ohio 44115
Winous-Point Building
1250 Euclid Avenue

Detroit, Michigan 48226
Book Building
1257-1259 Washington Blvd.

Los Angeles, California 90014
510 West 6th Street

Minneapolis, Minnesota 55402
124 South 7th Street
Northstar Center

New York, New York 10019
680 Fifth Avenue

Philadelphia, Pennsylvania 19102
Suite 1309
3 Benjamin Franklin Parkway

Pittsburgh, Pennsylvania 15222
1001-1003 Jenkins Arcade
Liberty and Fifth Avenues

San Francisco, California 94104
600 Market Street, Suite 2300
Crocker Plaza

Seattle, Washington 98101
Suite 1117
Plaza 600
600 Stewart Street

Washington, D.C. 20036
N.A.B. Building
1771 N. Street N.W.

camping in mexico

The Mexican National Park system does not provide facilities for campsites, and camping by the side of the road or on beaches is not recommended. With persistence, however, you can make arrangements to camp in Mexico and have an exciting trip which could include the tropics, snow-capped volcanoes, pre-Hispanic ruins of great cultures including the Mayans and the Aztecs, and gay fiestas which are the heart and soul of Mexico.

101

One of the ways in which young people camping in a group can tour Mexico comfortably is through the American Youth Hostel tours, if you are fourteen years or older. Complete information can be obtained from their office at 20 West Seventeenth Street, New York, New York 10011, or at one of their twenty-six Councils located throughout the United States in major cities. Check your phone book to see if there is a Council listed under American Youth Hostels.

The second is by planning a trip with adult advisors, or family, using the facilities of the Kampgrounds of America (KOA), a private, franchised organization which is opening KOAMEX Kampamentos throughout Mexico. Write for their booklet *Camping in Mexico* and their Directory. The address is Box 1138, Billings, Montana 59103. They will also give you a listing of quality camping accommodations in areas where there are no KOAs as yet. One of the difficulties is that most other camping facilities are in trailer parks, and it is difficult to learn by letter correspondence whether there are tentsites or only trailer accommodations.

102

BORDER CROSSING

TOURIST CARD

To cross the border, you need a tourist card which can be obtained without charge. The card is good for 180 days, and you must keep it with you at all times. You do not need a passport or visa. If you are a young man over eighteen years old, carry your draft card with you.

To get a tourist card, one must show either a birth or baptismal certificate, or a notarized voter's card. If you are under fifteen and traveling with your parents, you are covered by their card but your birth certificate must be shown.

If traveling in an informal group with adult supervision other than parents, in order to get your tourist card you need to show a notarized letter signed by both parents or guardians authorizing the trip as well as a birth or baptismal certificate. If you are traveling with one parent, you must have a notarized letter from the other parent.

Educational and cultural trips for groups of children under fifteen are permitted for up to sixty days, provided that one authorized person from the institution organizing the trip accompanies them and presents, along with birth certificates, **103** a notarized letter in duplicate signed by both parents or guardians authorizing the trip.

Tourist cards may be obtained before reaching the border through Mexican Consulates, Mexican Government Tourist Department offices, and from airlines and railroads serving Mexico. For application by mail, obtain Form DT-54 from one of the above offices, complete and sign it. Return with correct papers and a stamped self-addressed envelope.

Naturalized citizens need either a passport or their naturalization certificate. Alien residents of the United States can obtain a tourist permit only at Mexican Consulates in the United States.

AUTOMOBILES

The following should be helpful to your adult advisor:

You need an auto permit for car and trailer. You receive the permit by presenting the motor vehicle registration certificate for both car and trailer, and driver's license. These permits are good for six months.

104 If the car or trailer has a loan on it, you must have a notarized letter from the loanholder authorizing you to take the vehicle out of the country. If it is not your own, you should have a letter of permission from the owner, or the rental contract.

If you are visiting border areas of Mexico for seventy-two hours or less, you do not need a tourist card or auto permit.

Declare anything you take into the country. Otherwise you may have to pay duty when you recross the border.

VACCINATIONS

Vaccinations are no longer required, unless you've just returned to America or Canada from another foreign country within the last fourteen days, or are planning to go on to Central or South America. However, it's always a good idea to have your immunizations up to date: polio, tetanus, typhoid and paratyphoid. On re-entering the United States, you must show proof of smallpox vaccination.

YOUR DOG

You can take your dog to Mexico. Any pet must have a certificate (in duplicate) from a veterinarian stating that the animal is in good health and that it has been inoculated against rabies within the past six months. The certificate must be visaed by a Mexican Consulate and will cost about $4.00. One copy of the certificate is needed for the Mexican Government upon entering, and one for the United States Government upon returning. Without this certificate, you will have to put your pet in quarantine.

common sense

Plan your trip so that you can get where you want to go, do what you want to do, without being overly tired. Try, in other words, to stop your heavy activity before you reach extreme weariness.

106

Use your common sense, as if you were at home, and avoid sunburn, heat exhaustion, and overexposure in general.

Sleeping out under the stars is a lovely thought. But better to enjoy the wonders of nature before you go to sleep, and then retire to your tent with flap closed.

first-aid kit

Buy the best first-aid kit available. One that is very complete is called the Sportsman's First-Aid Kit. Most camping or drugstores carry them. A useful kit should have:

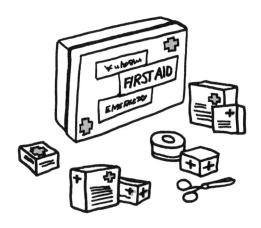

Adhesive bandages
Adhesive tape
Antiseptic ointment
Aspirin
Burn ointment
Gauze
Laxative
Scissors
Snake-bite kit
Soda mint tablets
Tweezers
Water-purification tablets

The following items are not usually in a kit but they are important to your well-being as well as your health. Whether or not you take them depends upon where you are going to be and how much space is available for packing.

Anti-chapping ointment
Baking soda
Boric acid
Cotton swabs
Cough syrup or drops

Diarrhea medication
Disinfectant
Epsom salts
Eye dropper
Insect-bite lotion and repellent
Rubbing alcohol
Special individual medication

first-aid course

Try to take a first-aid course. It may be offered in your neighborhood by the American Red Cross, your school, recreation commission, or Scout troop.

If you cannot enroll in a course, buy and read *The First Aid Textbook* published by the American National Red Cross, 150 Amsterdam Avenue, New York, New York 10023, or through your local chapter. The cost is $1.05 plus mailing. Take it with you on your trip.

108

insecticides

Buy a general repellent and follow instructions.

Equally important, as mentioned in Chapter 5, choose a site away from trees and stagnant water where insects gather.

animals

Before we talk about specific animals, here are some rules of behavior which should help keep animals *away* from your campsite, and out of your tent.

1. Store food properly in hamper or cooler and keep your campsite clean.
2. Replace equipment in box or bag after using. As you may know, it's the salt left on handles from human perspiration that makes them appealing to raccoons.
3. Keep the flap closed on your tent at all times.
4. Keep your dog on a leash directly in front of your tent at night.

Back to the title of this chapter, it's a matter of common sense. Treat strange animals while camping as you would strange dogs at home—leave them alone, *quietly* alone.

The rules of the National Park Service, which can be applied to all parks and camping areas, are very clear:

> "Do not feed wild animals. Injuries to campers by bears or other animals are usually due to the campers, attempts to feed them. Observe the animals but do not interfere with them. Food supplies should be locked up or hung out of reach."

About specific animals, here's some additional advice.

Bears—if a bear should come into your camp, walk slowly away or into your tent and close the flap.

Deer—if deer are eating nearby, leave them alone.

Porcupine and Raccoons—stay quiet and they will eventually go away.

Skunks—stay quiet and hope for the best. Should you be hit by the spray, here's what to do:

1. Wash yourself with soap and water, followed by a mild vinegar rinse.
2. Wash clothing or sleeping bags with vinegar or ammonia solution. Such action is seldom

effective, and usually you end up burying the items.

3. Rub corn meal into your dog's fur to absorb the oil from the spray.

4. Put all items in the fresh air and stay there yourself.

111

Snakes are not as great a danger as you might think. Of the three hundred varieties, four are poisonous—the rattlesnake, the copperhead, the coral snake, and the water moccasin. Snakes are shy, and they prefer to stay away from you. Most bites occur when hikers accidentally step on snakes, particularly in rocky areas.

Here are precautions to take:

1. Ask the park superintendent or ranger if there are places to be avoided.
2. Wear boots and trousers that cover boot tops.
3. Stay on trails.
4. Do not reach into animal holes.
5. Snakes are most active at night so stay close to your campfire, and if you find it necessary to walk about, stay on paths.
6. Do not walk barefoot, wear shoes or boots.
7. Read your First-Aid Textbook carefully and memorize the instructions in the Snake-Bite Kit.

poisonous plants

Learn the plants that cause serious trouble. Avoid them.

Poison Ivy is a vine or a low shrub. The three shiny leaves in a cluster are dark shiny green in summer, red or orange in fall. Berries are white in early spring and fall, green in between.

Poison Oak is a cousin of poison ivy with the same characteristics except the leaves are oak-shaped and fuzzy underneath.

Poison Sumac is a shrub or small tree. The leaves are smooth edged, and there are a number on each stem, usually seven to thirteen.

poison ivy

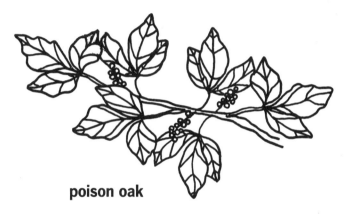

poison oak

poison sumac

list of things you will need

A checklist is a necessity. The word itself reminds you to *make* a list of things needed, and *check* your supplies by the list before you leave.

114

Here are suggestions. Don't consider this as final because camping is a very personal experience. You will have items to add and things to take away.

Shelter
Ground cloth or tarp
Tent
Tent stakes, poles, ropes, or frame

Sleeping Gear

Air mattress or polyester foam
Air pump and patch kit, if using air mattress
Sleeping bag or blanket bag

Tools

Ax
Folding saw
Hammer
Light digging tool, trowel, or shovel
Pliers
Pocket knife or Swiss Army knife
Screwdriver

Personal

Chapstick
Comb
Facial tissue
Hairbrush
Hand lotion
Mirror
Shampoo
Soap and plastic box or bag
Toilet tissue
Toothbrush and powder or paste
Towel and washcloths (2)

115

Miscellaneous

Alarm clock
Broom, small one to clean up camp
Clothespins
Compass
Dark glasses
Duffel bag or substitute
Flashlights, extra batteries and bulb (Mallory is the brand
   name of a flashlight that is small but strong.)

Knapsack and canteen, or thermos
Lanterns and extra generator or mantles
Needle and thread
Rope for clothesline
Rubber bands
Safety matches, 2 boxes at least
Safety pins
Scissors
Stamped postcards and pen or pencil
Wallet
Washbasin
Watch
Waterproof box for matches
Water-purification tablets
Woodsman's Emergency Kit
Zipper lubricant

Clothing
Clothing for special activities
Gloves
Head and neck scarves
Hiking shoes
Jacket
Lightweight shoes
Raingear
Shower sandals
Shirts (1 long sleeved, 1 heavy, 1 light)
Slacks
Sleepwear
Socks—lightweight and heavy
Sweater
Swimsuit
Underwear
Wide-brimmed hat

Cooking
Aluminum-foil disposable baking pans
Aluminum foil, heavy duty

Bags, heavy plastic or nylon, for storage of foods and liquids
Butter keeper
Can opener, 4-way with corkscrew preferably
Charcoal and starter (preferably powder, not liquid)
Chemical ice
Chopping board, small
Corn popper
Dishpans, 2
Egg beater or whisk
Egg carrier
Fish scaler
Food hamper, thick bag or metal hamper which can be closed
    tightly
Frying pan
Fuel, if needed
Garbage bags
Grill or portable cooking stove (see Chapter 6)
Ice chest
Juice container
Liquid soap
Measuring cup and spoons
Paper or disposable plastic ware
    bowls
    cups
    knives, forks, spoons
    napkins
    plates
    towels
Plastic wrap
Saucepans, 1 large and 1 small
Skewers
Soap pads
Sponges
Teakettle
Thermos, regular and wide mouth
Tools—long-handled
    spoon
    fork

ladle
spatula
tongs
Tools—regular
    multipurpose knife
    paring knife
    vegetable parer
    wooden mixing spoon
Water carrier

Recreational

Binoculars
Camera and film
Fishing tackle with rod in metal or plastic case
Magnifying glass
Notebook
Playing cards

for more information

From the Superintendent of Documents,
U. S. Government Printing Office,
Washington, D.C. 20402

Backpacking in the National Forest Wilderness ($.25)
Back Country Travel in the National Park System ($.35)
Camping in the National Park System ($.25)
Camping, The National Forests
National Parks and Landmarks ($.60)
National Forest Vacations ($.30)

From the National Park Service,
Washington, D.C. 20240

Campground Director of the National Parks (free)

From the U. S. Geological Survey,
Washington, D.C. 20242

Topographic maps and some wilderness areas

From the Bureau of Sport Fisheries and Wildlife,
Washington, D.C. 20240

Details of wilderness lands in the National Wildlife
Refuges and Range

From the Regional Forester, Forest Service, for information
on National Forests and National Grasslands in each area as
follows:

Alaska Region
P. O. Box 1628
Juneau, Alaska 99801
Pacific Northwest Region
P. O. Box 3623
Portland, Oregon 97208
California Region
630 Sansome Street
San Francisco, California 94111
Northern Region
Federal Building
Missoula, Montana 59801
Intermountain Region
324 25th Street
Ogden, Utah 84401
Rocky Mountain Region
Federal Center, Building 85
Denver, Colorado 80225
Southwestern Region
517 Gold Avenue S.W.
Albuquerque, New Mexico 87101
Eastern Region
633 West Wisconsin Avenue
Milwaukee, Wisconsin 53202
Southern Region
50 Seventh Street N.E.
Atlanta, Georgia 30323

From American Forest Institute,
    1835 K Street N.W.,
    Washington, D.C. 20006

    Private Forest Land Recreation List in the United States

From Woodall Publishing Co.,
    500 Hyacinth Place,
    Highland Park, Illinois 60035

    Woodall's 1971 *Trailering Parks and Campgrounds Directory, a Complete Guide.* ($5.95)

general information

American Youth Hostels
National Headquarters
20 West Seventeenth Street
New York, New York 10011

Appalachian Mountain Club
5 Joy Street
Boston, Massachusetts 02108

Appalachian Trail Conference
1916 Sunderland Place, N.W.
Washington, D.C. 36200

Campfire Club of America
19 Rector Street
New York, New York 10006

Girl Scouts of U.S.A.
830 3rd Ave.—Program Dept.
New York, New York 10022

Boy Scouts of America
U.S. Highway #1
North Brunswick, N.J. 08902

122

National Campers and
Hikers Association
7172 Transit Road
Buffalo, New York 14221

National Audubon Society
1130 Fifth Avenue
New York, New York 10028

Sierra Club
1050 Mills Tower
270 Bush Street
San Francisco, Cal. 94104

The Wilderness Society
729 Fifteenth Street, N.W.
Washington, D.C. 20005

Camping Magazines
Better Camping
Campfire Chatter
Camping Guide
Camping Journal

Camping Catalogues
Camp and Trail Outfitters
112 Chambers Street
New York, New York 10007

Morsan
2485 Route 33
Union, New Jersey 07803

Recreational Equipment
Co-op Inc.
1525 11th Avenue
Seattle, Washington 98122

Private Campgrounds
National Campground
Owners Association
Bradford Woods
Martinsville, Indiana 46151

Kampgrounds of
America (KOA)
P. O. Box 1138
Billings, Montana 59103

123

index

Addresses for more information, 17, 20, 25, 89, 99–100, 102, 119–23. *See also* specific aspects, organizations.

Air Mattresses, 37

American Youth Hostel, 13; and Mexican camping, 101–2

Animals (*see also* Dogs; Pets); strange, precautions and, 109–12

Applesauce pudding (recipe), 77

Automobiles (*see also* Recreation vehicles; Trailers): and Canadian camping, 98; and Mexican camping, 104

Backpacking, 87–92; meaning of, 87; planning for, 88–89; seasons for, 88; supplies and equipment for, 90–92

Barbecued beef on bun (recipe), 74

Barbecued Spanish rice with meat (recipe), 74–75

Beans and pork with canned meat, 77

Bears, 110

"Beef Jerky," 63

Beef on bun, barbecued (recipe), 74

Beef sandwiches, 74, 78

Bicycle riding, 15

Blankets: airing, 47; as substitutes for sleeping bags, 38–39

Boots. *See* Footwear (boots; shoes)

Border crossings: Canadian camping and, 89, 99; Mexican camping and, 102–4

Bread and bread products, 85. *See also* specific kinds

Camper's punch (recipe), 75

Campfires, 50–57; building, 54–55; Canadian camping and, 97; cooking and, 50–57 (*see also* Cooking, camp); fuel for, 19; grills, 55; hunter's (trapper's) fire, 51; national forests and, 23; national parks and, 19; open-fire, 50–51; portable stoves, 55–57; preparations and precautions, 49, 53; rock fire, 51–52; safety precautions and, 49, 53; trench fire, 52

Campgrounds, 16–19 (*see also* Campsites; specific aspects); camp life and, 40–49; commercial, 25; county and regional parks, 24; national forests, 20–23; national parks, 16–19; selecting, 9, 11–12, 16–19; sleeping bags, 35–39; state parks, 23–24; tents, 26–34; types, 16

Camping in the National Park System, 17, 19

Campsites, 41–49 (*see also* Campgrounds; specific aspects); breaking up, 47–49; Canadian camping, 96; cooking and (*see* Cooking, camp); making it livable, 42–45; packing and, 48; safety and, 49, 109–12 (*see also* Safety precautions); sanitation at, 41, 44–47, 49; seashore camping and, 94; selecting, 41–42; setting up, 41–45; strange animals and precautions, 109–12; while there, 45–47

Canada, camping in, 95–100; border crossing, 98, 99; campsites, 96; fees, 96; fishing, 98; group tenting sites, 97; pets, 97, 98; travel service, 99

Canned foods, use of, 82–83

Caramel pudding (recipe), 76–77

Cars. *See* Automobiles

Cereals, use of, 65, 83

Charcoal, use of, 19

Chicken, canned, use of, 83

Chicken rice (recipe), 76

Chocolate bar, tropical, 63

Chocolate-peanut fondue (recipe), 78

Cleanliness (sanitation): at campsite, 41, 44–47, 49; and eating accessories, 59–60; garbage disposal, 46; and meals, 45; personal habits, 47; and sleeping bags, 37; and tents, 34

Clothing (*see also* specific kinds): airing, 38, 47; backpacking and, 90–92; checklist of, 116; sleeping, 38

Commercial campgrounds, 16, 25; addresses for information, 25, 123; reservations, 25; types, 25

Cooking, camp, 50–57, 58–59, 62–65; campfires and, 52–57 (*see also* Campfires); checklist of supplies, 116–17; eating accessories, 59; emergency food, 63; equipment and supplies, 58–61, 62–65, 116–18; grocery list, 82–86; planning meals, 62–65 (*see also* Food); pots and pans, 58; recipes, 74–81; refrigeration, 60–61; suggested menus, 66–81

Copperhead snakes, 111

Coral snakes, 111

County and regional parks, 24

Dairy products, use of, 85. *See also* specific kinds

Deer, 110

Deviled ham-peanut butter sandwich filling (recipe), 79

Dogs, 15, 109; Canadian camping and, 97, 99; Mexican camping and, 105

Drinking water, 23

Drinks (recipes): fruit punches, 75, 79; high-protein, 81

Eating (*see also* Cooking, camp; Food): emergency foods, 63; grocery list, 82–86; planning meals, 62–65; suggested menus, 66–81; supplies and equipment, 14–15, 58–61, 62–65, 82–86

Eggs, fresh and powdered, use of, 64

Emergency foods, 63

Equipment. *See* Supplies and equipment; specific kinds, uses

Fees: Canadian camping, 96; national forests, 21–22; national parks, 17, 18; state parks, 24

Fire(s). *See* Campfires

First-aid course, 108

First-aid kit, 107–8

First-Aid Textbook, 108

Fish, canned, use of, 83

Fishing equipment and regulations, Canadian camping and, 98

Foam mattresses, use of, 37

Food (meals), 14–15, 62–65 (*see also* specific kinds, recipes); backpacking and, 88, 89, 90; buying and packing, 62–63; camp cooking, 50–57, 58–61, 62–65 (*see also* Cooking, camp); campfires and, 50–57 (*see also* Campfires); cleaning up (sanitation) and, 45, 46; emergency, 63; equipment and supplies, 14–15, 58–61, 62–65, 82–86, 116–18; grocery lists, 14–15, 82–86; planning, 62–65; recipes,

125

Food (*cont.*)
    74–81; refrigeration, 60–61;
    suggested menus, 14, 66–87
    (*see also* Menus)
Footwear (boots; shoes), 10, 91–
    92
Franchise campgrounds, 25
Fruit-peanut butter sandwich
    (recipe), 81
Fruit punches (recipes), 75, 79,
    81
Fruits and juices, use of, 82–83,
    86 ,
Fuel, and campfires, 19

Garbage disposal, 46
Gasoline camp stoves, 56–57
Glazed meat cubes (recipe), 80
Grills, lightweight, 55
Groceries, suggested lists of, 14–
    15, 82–86
Group tenting sites, 97

Ham: deviled, and peanut butter
    sandwich filling (recipe), 78;
    smoked, use of, 65
High-protein drink (recipe), 81
High-protein sandwich spread
    (recipe), 80–81
Hiking, 15, 87. *See also* Back-
    packing
Hunter's (trapper's) fire, 51

Ice, and food refrigeration, 60–61
Insect repellents, 109

Jerky, beef, 63
Juices and fruits, use of, 82–83,
    86

Kampgrounds of America (KOA),
    25, 102
Kool-Aid fruit punch, 75, 79, 81

Maps, 14
Margarine, use of, 64
Mattresses, sleeping, 37
Meals. *See* Food (meals)
Meat cubes, glazed (recipe), 80
Meat meal recipes, 74–75, 77, 78,
    79, 80. *See also* specific
    kinds, recipes

Meats, on grocery list, 83, 85
Medical (first-aid) kit, 107–8
Menus, 5, 14, 66–81 (*see also*
    Food; specific foods, rec-
    ipes); grocery list and, 82–
    86; planning, 14, 62–65; rec-
    ipes, 74–81; suggested, 66–
    81
Mexico, camping in, 101–5; Amer-
    ican Youth Hostel tours, 101–
    2; automobiles and, 104;
    border crossing and, 102–4;
    dogs and, 105; KOA and,
    102; tourist cards and, 102–
    4; vaccinations and, 105
Milk, non-fat dry, use of, 63–64,
    83

National forests, camping in, 16,
    20–23: backpacking, 87–92;
    campfires, 23; facilities, 21;
    fees, 21; length of stay, 22;
    reservations, 21; season
    length, 22; supplies, 23; trail-
    ers, 22; water, 23
National Forest Vacations, 20
National parks, camping in, 16–
    19: backpacking, 19, 87–92;
    Canadian camping and, 95–
    100; fees, 18, 96; fuel and
    fires, 19; length of stay, 19;
    recreation vehicles, 18; reser-
    vations, 18; seashore camp-
    ing and, 93–94
Non-fat dry milk, use of, 63–64,
    83

*Off on the Right Foot: A Guide to
    Proper Wilderness Use*, 89
Open-fire camp cooking, 5
Optimus camping stove, 57

Packing, 48
Pans. *See* Pots and pans
Peanut butter and deviled ham
    sandwich filling (recipe), 79
Peanut butter-fruit sandwich (rec-
    ipe), 81
Peanut-chocolate fondue (recipe),
    78

"Pemmican Woodsman Emergency Kit," 63
Pets, 15, 109; Canadian camping and, 97, 99; Mexican camping and, 105
Planning the trip, 13–15, 106–12 (*see also* specific aspects, locations); backpacking and, 88–89; camp cooking and food, 14–15, 62–65, 82–86 (*see also* Cooking, camp; Food); campgrounds and campsites, 16–19, 40–49 (*see also* Campgrounds; Campsites; specific aspects); camp life, 40–49; equipment, 14, 114–18 (*see also* Supplies and equipment; specific kinds, uses); maps, 14; pets, 15, 109 (*see also* Pets); safety precautions, 106–12; sleeping bags, 35–39; tents, 26–34; time schedule, 15; training and, 15; where to go and stay, 14, 16–19, 20–25
Plants, poisonous, 112
Poison ivy, 112
Poison oak, 112
Poisonous plants, 112
Poison sumac, 112
Polyester foam mattresses, use of, 37
Porcupines, 110
Pork and beans with canned meat, 77
Pots and pans, 58–59
Private campgrounds, 25 (*see also* Commercial campgrounds); addresses for information, 25, 123
Pudding recipes, 76–77; applesauce, 77; caramel, 76–77

Raccoons, 109, 110
Rattlesnakes, 111
Recreational supplies, checklist of, 118
Recreational vehicles, 18, 22
Refrigeration of food, 60–61
Regional parks. *See* County and regional parks

Reservations: commercial campgrounds, 25; national forests, 21; national parks, 18
Rice, chicken (recipe), 76
Rice with meat, barbecued (recipe), 74–75
Road maps, 14
Rock fire, 51–52

Safety precautions, 106–12; and animals (strange), 109–12; and campfires, 49, 53; first-aid course, 108; first-aid kit, 107–8; insect repellents, 109; and poisonous plants, 112; and snakes, 111–12
Sandwich spread, high-protein (recipe), 80–81
Seashore camping, 93–94; campsites, 94; supplies, 94
Shelter equipment, checklist of, 114. *See also* specific kinds, uses
Shoes. *See* Footwear (boots; shoes)
Skunks, precautions and treatment, 110–11
Sleeping bags, 35–39; airing, 38, 47; fabrics, 36; fillings, 36; hoods, 37; substitutes for, 38–39; zippers, 36
Sleeping gear, checklist of, 115. *See also* specific kinds
Snakes, poisonous and non-poisonous, precautions against, 111–12
Spanish rice with meat, barbecued (recipe), 74–75
Sportsman's First-Aid Kit, 107
State parks, camping in, 16, 23–24: fees, 24
Sterno stove, 55–56
Stoves, portable, 55–57
Supplies and equipment, 9, 12, 14, 114–18 (*see also* specific items, kinds, uses); backpacking and, 88, 89, 90–92; campfires and, 52–57; checklists of, 114–18; choosing, 12, 14; clothing, 116; cook-

Supplies and equipment (*cont.*) ing and, 52–57, 58–61, 62–65, 116–18; first-aid, 107–8; grocery, 82–86; personal, 115–16; safety precautions and, 107–12; seashore camping and, 94; shelter, 114 (*see also* Tents); sleeping gear, 115 (*see also* specific kinds); tools, 115, 117–18

SVEA 123 gasoline stove, 56

Tents, 26–30; buying, 26–28; care of, 34, 48; floor, 29; placement at campsite, 32, 43; putting up, 30, 34; and seashore camping, 94; stakes, lines, and poles, 29–30; ventilation, 28; water repellency, 28

Tinder, and building of campfire, 53, 54

Toasted bread, 64–65

Tools, checklist of, 115, 117–18

Tourist cards, Mexican camping and, 102–4

Trailering Parks and Campgrounds Directory, 25

Trailers, use of, 22

Trench fire, 52

"Tropical Chocolate Bar," 63

U. S. Geological Survey, 14

Vaccinations: Canadian camping and, 99; Mexican camping and, 105

Vegetables: canned, use of, 83, 86; on grocery list, canned and frozen, 86

Vehicles: *See* Automobiles; Recreational vehicles; Trailers

Water: drinking, 23; washing, 59–60

Water moccasin snakes, 111

Wilderness Society, 89

Zippers, sleeping bags and, 36, 37

128